The Usborne
Big Book of Stars & Planets

Written by Emily Bone
Illustrated by Fabiano Fiorin
Designed by Stephen Wright

Space expert: Stuart Atkinson

Our planet

We live on Planet Earth, a huge, round lump of rock floating in space.

A layer of gases, called the **atmosphere**, gives us **air** to breathe, and makes sure we don't get too hot or too cold.

Earth is a very wet planet. Huge **seas** and **oceans** cover almost **three-quarters** of the Earth's surface.

The white swirls are **clouds**. Rain falls from the clouds, which makes plants grow.

The green and brown shapes are **land**.

There are thousands of man-made things in space. **Satellites** are **spacecraft** that fly around the Earth to gather and send information.

The Moon is a rocky ball that travels around the Earth. We can see the Moon in our night sky.

Weather satellites help to forecast the weather.

Global Positioning System (GPS) satellites create maps and send directions to our phones, computers and vehicles.

The light patches are mountain ranges on the Moon's surface.

Television satellites send television signals across the world.

These are **meteors** – tiny space rocks that burn up in the Earth's atmosphere.

Over **seven billion people** live on Earth. The lights from big **cities** can be seen from space.

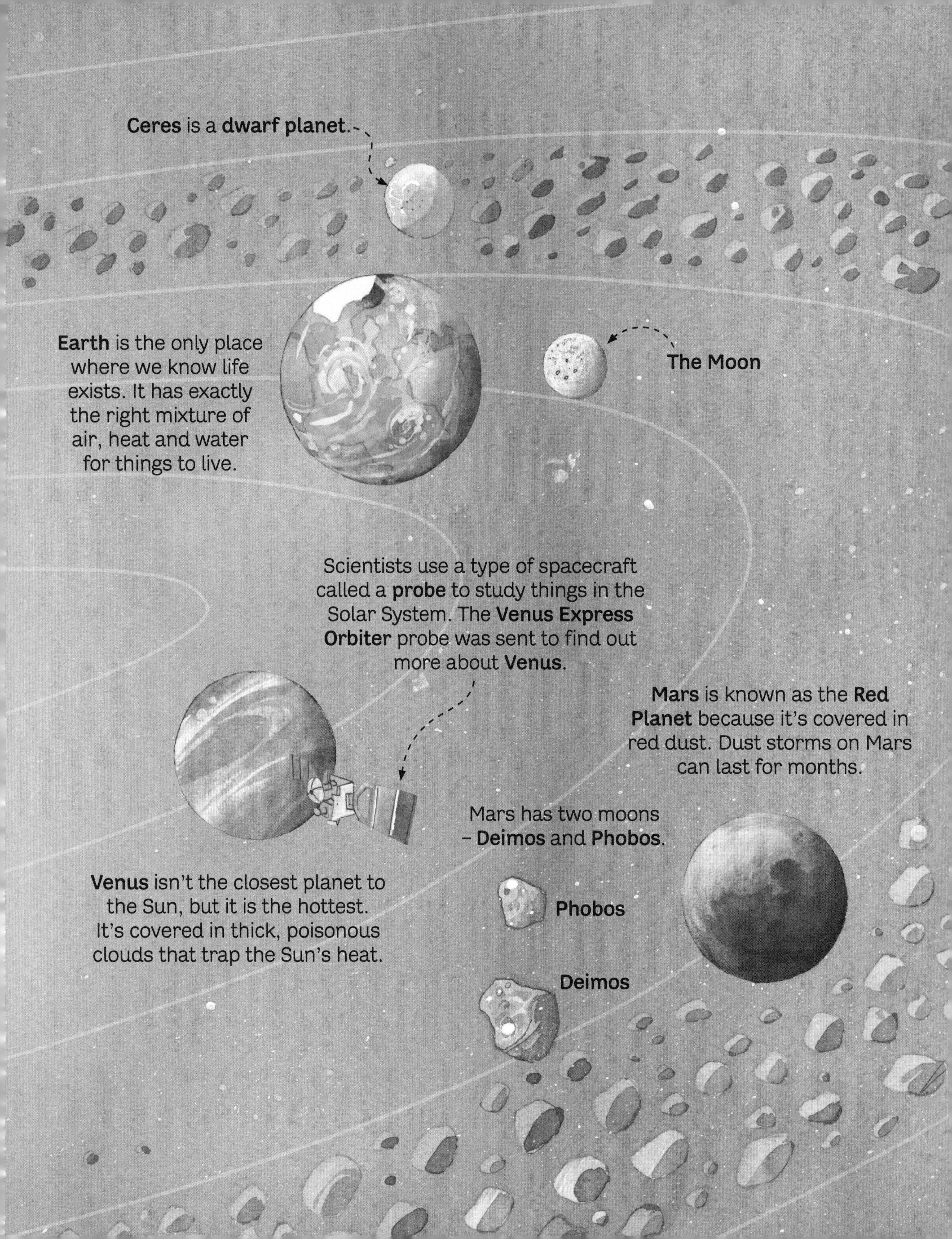

Ceres is a **dwarf planet**.

Earth is the only place where we know life exists. It has exactly the right mixture of air, heat and water for things to live.

The Moon

Scientists use a type of spacecraft called a **probe** to study things in the Solar System. The **Venus Express Orbiter** probe was sent to find out more about **Venus**.

Mars is known as the **Red Planet** because it's covered in red dust. Dust storms on Mars can last for months.

Mars has two moons – **Deimos** and **Phobos**.

Venus isn't the closest planet to the Sun, but it is the hottest. It's covered in thick, poisonous clouds that trap the Sun's heat.

Phobos

Deimos

Sometimes, **asteroids** crash into each other, making them shoot off into space.

If an asteroid smashes into a planet's surface, it makes a deep hole, called a **crater**.

Mercury is the closest planet to the Sun. Its surface is very, very hot – four times hotter than boiling water.

These lines show the **orbits** of the planets – the paths they take around the Sun.

The Sun is an extremely hot and bright ball of gas, called a **star**. It's massive – over a million times bigger than **Earth**.

The Sun

The Solar System

The Earth is one of eight planets that move around a star called the Sun. The Sun and its planets are known as the Solar System.

A planet's **year** is the time it takes to go once around the Sun. Earth's year is 365 days.

As well as moving around the Sun, planets spin, too. A **day** is the time it takes for a planet to spin around once. Earth's day is just under 24 hours.

Mercury
Year: 88 Earth days
Day: 59 Earth days
Moons: 0

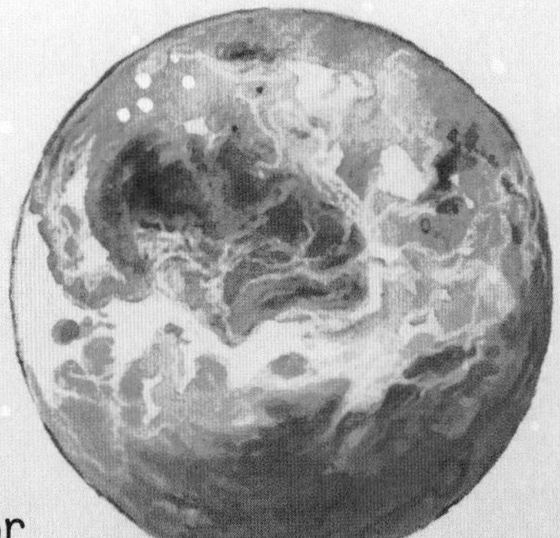

Venus
Year: 225 Earth days
Day: 117 Earth days
Moons: 0

Moons are rocky or icy lumps that travel around some planets.

Earth
Year: 365 Earth days
Day: 23 hours, 56 minutes
Moons: 1

Mars
Year: 687 Earth days
Day: 24 hours, 30 minutes
Moons: 2

All the planets on this page are mostly made of **rock**.

Eros

Ida

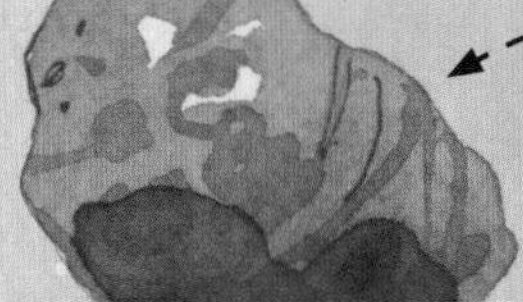

Asteroids are lumps of rock, metal or ice that move around in a big group called the **Asteroid Belt**. Most of the biggest ones have names.

The planets on this page are mostly made of **gas**.

Jupiter
Year: 12 Earth years
Day: 9 hours, 55 minutes
Moons: 67

Jupiter is **the biggest planet** in the Solar System.

Saturn
Year: 29.5 Earth years
Day: 10 hours, 42 minutes
Moons: 62

Gas planets have **rings** of dust, rock and ice circling them.

Saturn's rings are especially wide and impressive.

Uranus
Year: 84 Earth years
Day: 17 hours, 14 minutes
Moons: 27

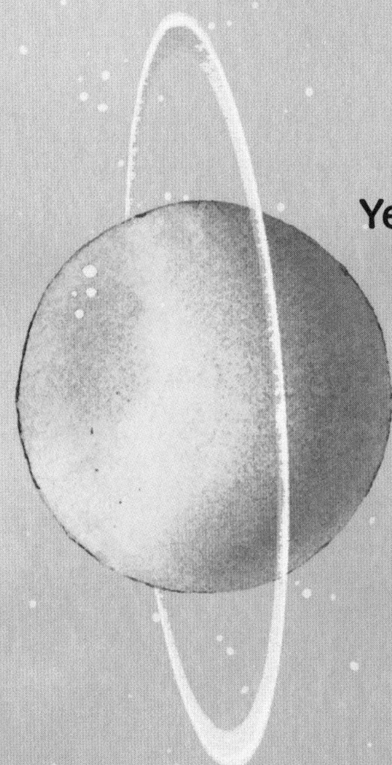

Neptune
Year: 165 Earth years
Day: 16 hours, 6 minutes
Moons: 14

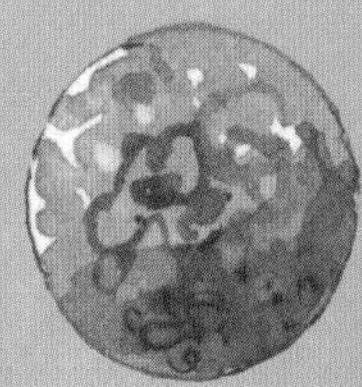

Dwarf planets are larger than asteroids, but smaller than planets. This is the dwarf planet **Pluto**.

The planets are actually very different sizes.
Here you can see how big they are compared to each other.

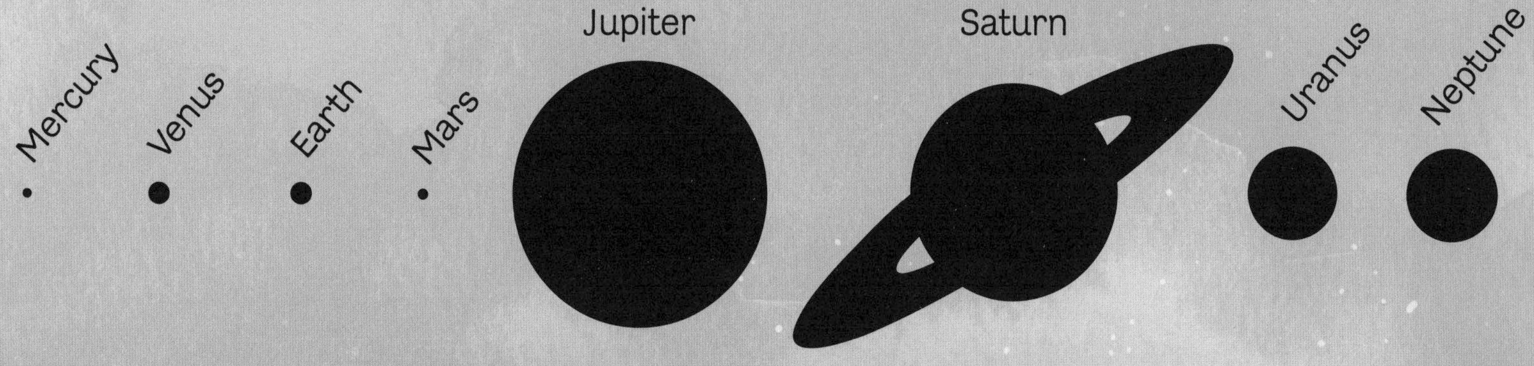

Comets are lumps of ice, dust and rock that melt and break up as they fly. Some have a bright 'tail' streaming out behind them.

Neptune is an extremely stormy planet. Its winds are 10 times faster than a spinning tornado on Earth.

Uranus spins as if it's been knocked on its side. This might be because a big asteroid crashed into the planet a long time ago.

Triton is Neptune's biggest moon.

Pluto

The **Kuiper Belt** is a band of icy rocks. Four **dwarf planets** have been discovered here.

Eris

Makemake

Haumea

Titania is Uranus's biggest moon.

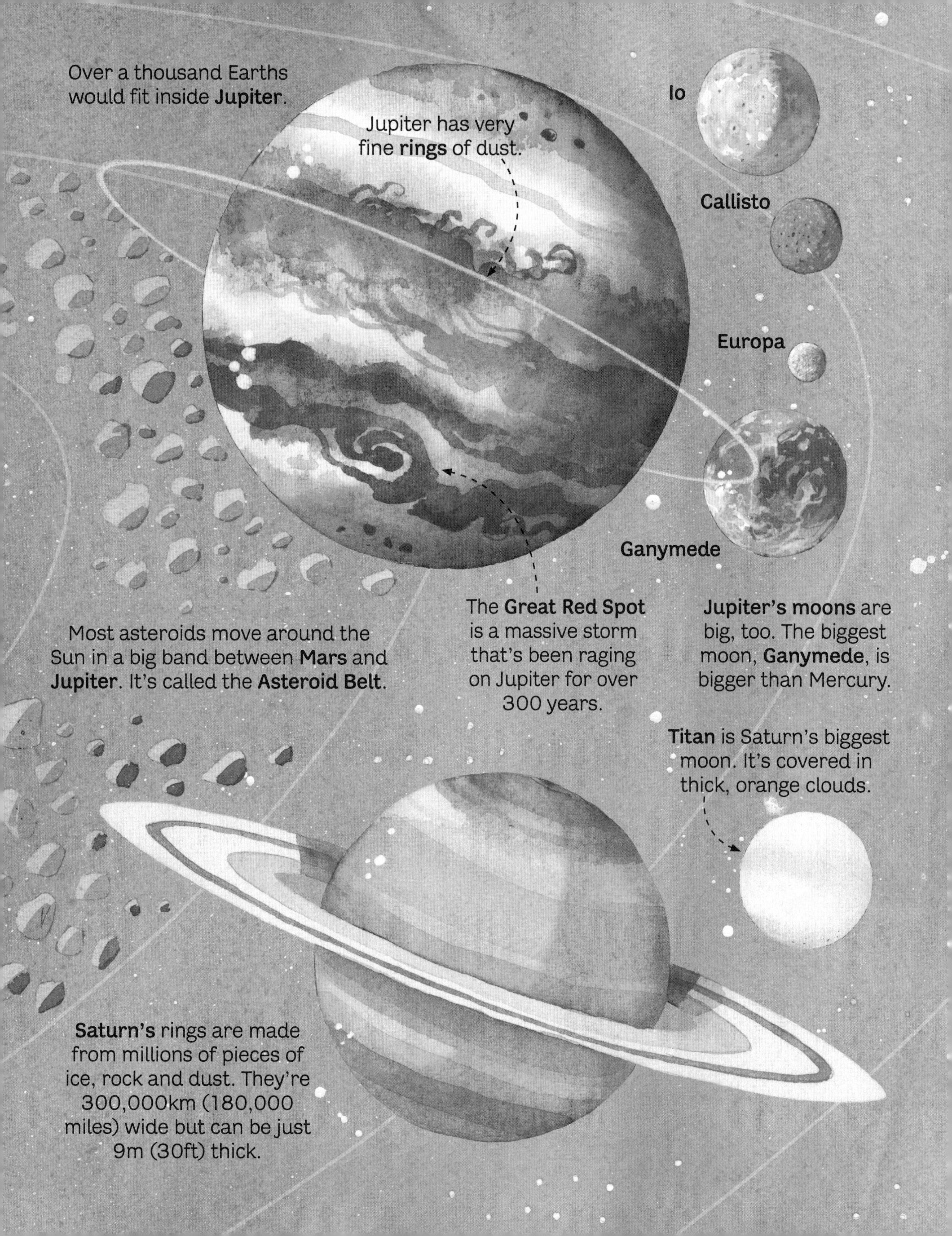

Over a thousand Earths would fit inside **Jupiter**.

Jupiter has very fine **rings** of dust.

Most asteroids move around the Sun in a big band between **Mars** and **Jupiter**. It's called the **Asteroid Belt**.

The **Great Red Spot** is a massive storm that's been raging on Jupiter for over 300 years.

Jupiter's moons are big, too. The biggest moon, **Ganymede**, is bigger than Mercury.

Titan is Saturn's biggest moon. It's covered in thick, orange clouds.

Saturn's rings are made from millions of pieces of ice, rock and dust. They're 300,000km (180,000 miles) wide but can be just 9m (30ft) thick.

The Sun

The Sun is a star, a massive ball of powerful, exploding gases. It gives the planets all their light and heat.

The surface of the Sun bubbles and churns. It's called the **chromosphere** and is 60 times hotter than boiling water.

Solar prominences are huge, fiery loops of gas that shoot out into space. They can be 20 times bigger than the Earth.

Solar tornadoes are fast, whirling funnels of gas. They're thousands of times bigger than tornadoes on Earth.
The **corona** is a layer of hot gases that surrounds the Sun. It's 5,000 times hotter than the surface below.
The Sun lets out a powerful stream of hot gases into space. This is called the **solar wind**.
A **fast riser** is a small, straight jet of gas that flies out of the Sun.

Super stars

There are billions and billions of stars in space. New stars explode into life from hot, swirling clouds of gas and dust, called *nebulae*.

Some galaxies are **merging**, which means they're slowly joining together to become one huge galaxy.

These are actually two **merging galaxies** called the **Mice Galaxies** because they look a little like mice with long tails.

We're part of the **Milky Way** galaxy, a **barred spiral galaxy** with arms coming out of a bar-shaped middle. Our Sun is just one of its stars.

This is the **Sombrero Galaxy**, named because it looks like a Mexican hat.

This is the **Orion Nebula**. It's the closest *nebula* to Earth.

Stars usually form in **star clusters**.

Gigantic galaxies

Galaxies are enormous groups of billions of stars, *nebulae*, gas and dust. They form spectacular shapes.

The outer layers of some dying stars puff away in clouds of gas. This is the **Cat's Eye Nebula** around a dying star.

The original star has turned into a small, heavy type of star called a **white dwarf**.

There are different types of stars.

Red dwarfs are the smallest and least powerful stars.

Yellow dwarfs produce a steady amount of light and heat. Our **Sun** is a yellow dwarf.

Sometimes, smaller stars circle bigger ones. These are called **binary stars.**

Blue supergiants are huge stars, thousands of times hotter and brighter than the Sun.

After millions and millions of years, a star's gas supply runs out and it starts to die.

A huge star, such as a blue supergiant, ends its life in a massive explosion, called a ***supernova***. This one is known as the **Crab Supernova** because it looks a little like a crab's shell.

This is an **irregular galaxy** called the **Cartwheel Galaxy**. It was made when two galaxies crashed into each other millions of years ago.

Spiral galaxies have arms that curve out of a bulging, bright middle. This is the **M74 Gemini** galaxy.

Elliptical galaxies are balls of old stars. This one is called **Messier 60**. It was the 60th galaxy discovered by Charles Messier, an 18th century astronomer.

The middle of the Milky Way looks very bright because there are lots of hot, glowing stars here.

Galaxies exist together in groups. The Milky Way's group is called the **Local Group**. It has over 30 galaxies in it.

Our **Solar System** is on one of the outer arms of the Milky Way.

The closest galaxy to the Milky Way is the **Andromeda Galaxy**.

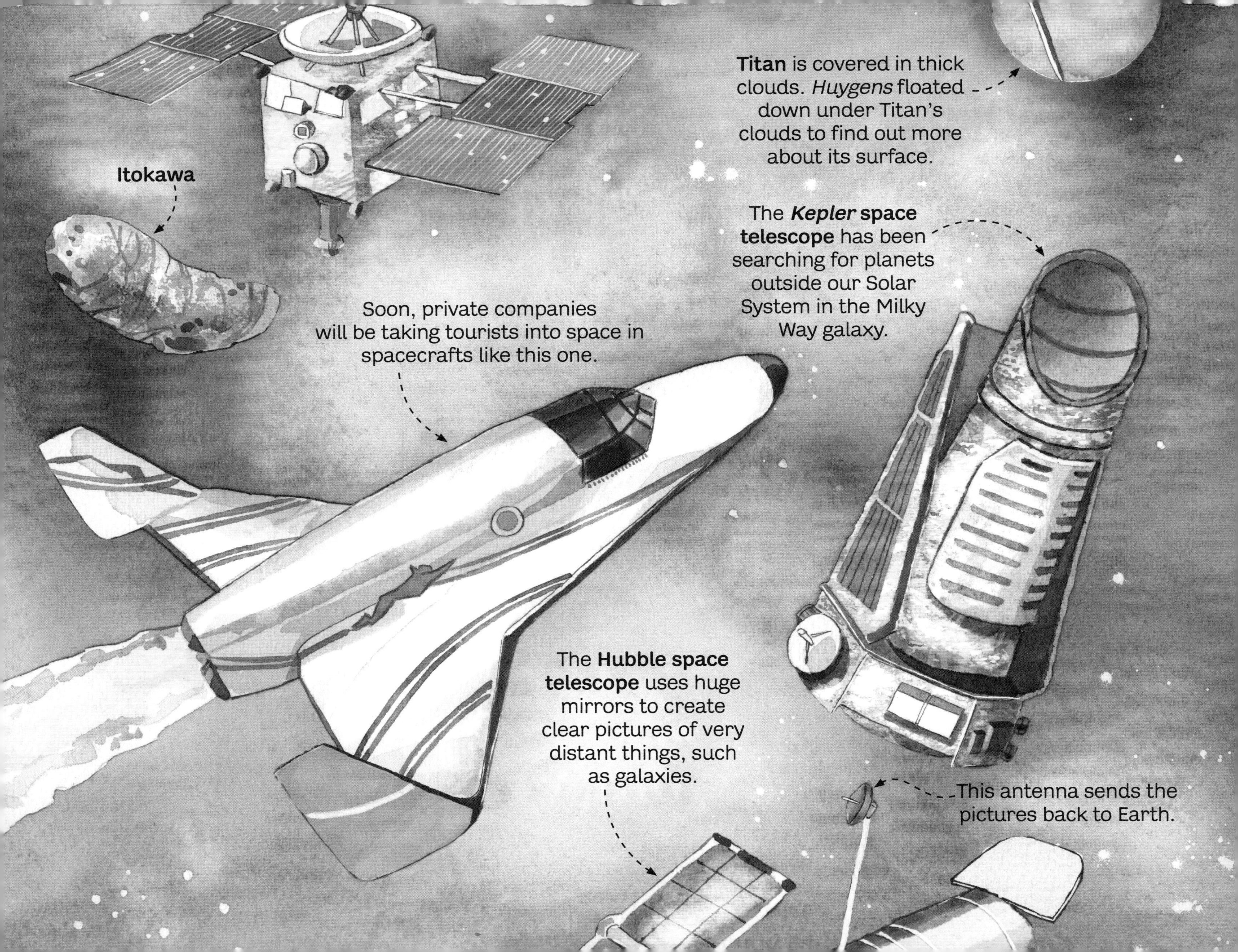
Itokawa
Soon, private companies will be taking tourists into space in spacecrafts like this one.
Titan is covered in thick clouds. *Huygens* floated down under Titan's clouds to find out more about its surface.
The ***Kepler* space telescope** has been searching for planets outside our Solar System in the Milky Way galaxy.
The **Hubble space telescope** uses huge mirrors to create clear pictures of very distant things, such as galaxies.
This antenna sends the pictures back to Earth.

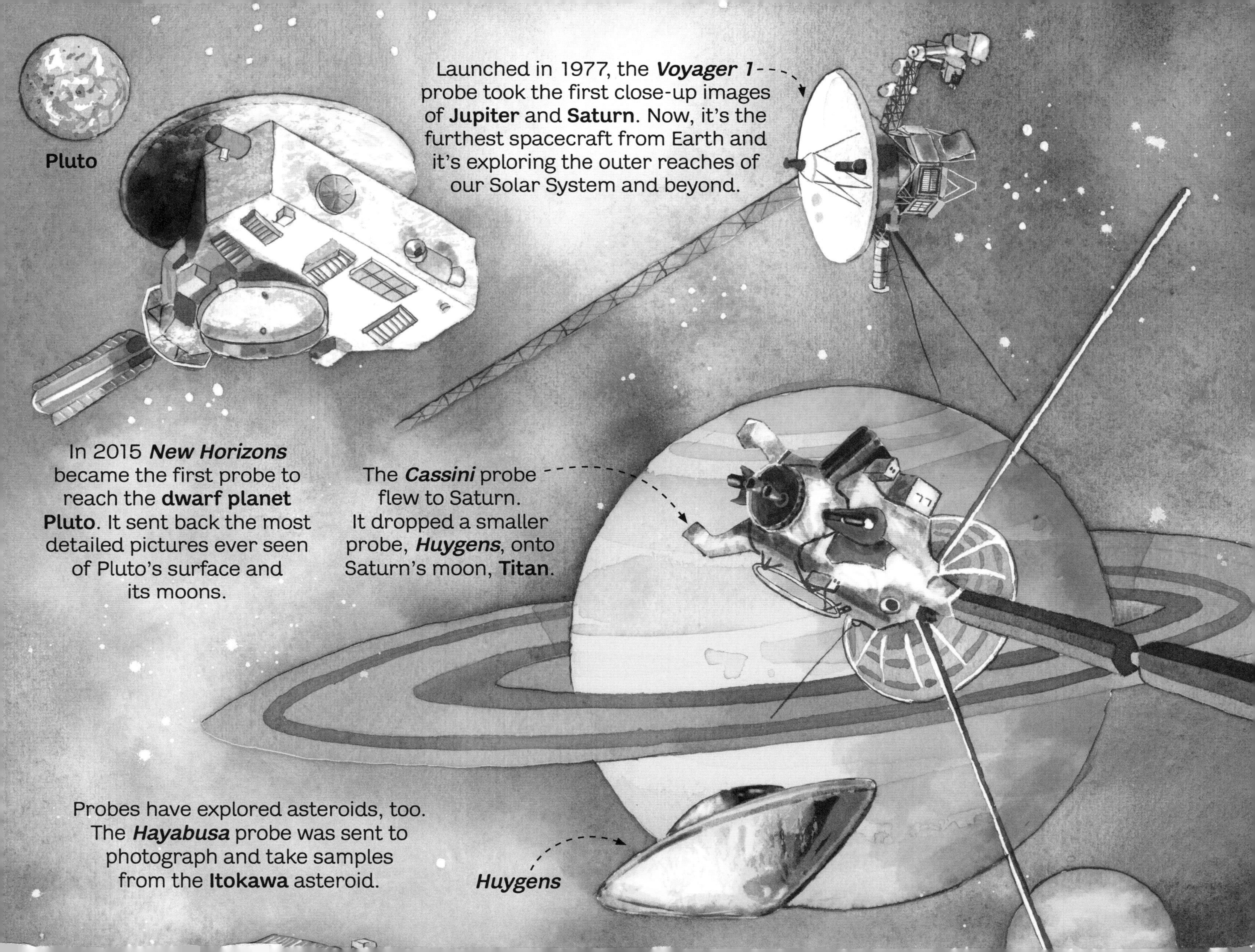

Launched in 1977, the ***Voyager 1*** probe took the first close-up images of **Jupiter** and **Saturn**. Now, it's the furthest spacecraft from Earth and it's exploring the outer reaches of our Solar System and beyond.

In 2015 ***New Horizons*** became the first probe to reach the **dwarf planet Pluto**. It sent back the most detailed pictures ever seen of Pluto's surface and its moons.

The ***Cassini*** probe flew to Saturn. It dropped a smaller probe, ***Huygens***, onto Saturn's moon, **Titan**.

Probes have explored asteroids, too. The ***Hayabusa*** probe was sent to photograph and take samples from the **Itokawa** asteroid.

Exploring space

Powerful rockets, spacecraft and telescopes help us find out about stars and planets.

The first spacecraft was ***Sputnik 1***, a Russian satellite launched in 1957. It flew around the Earth.

From 1969 to 1972, the US ***Apollo*** missions took astronauts to **the Moon**. The **Command Service Module (CSM)** spacecraft flew them there.

Probes use cameras and other instruments to study planets, moons and other things in space. The ***Cassini*** probe was launched in 1997.

Space telescopes orbit the Earth. They make things that are very far away look a lot bigger and clearer.

Astronauts wear protective spacesuits.

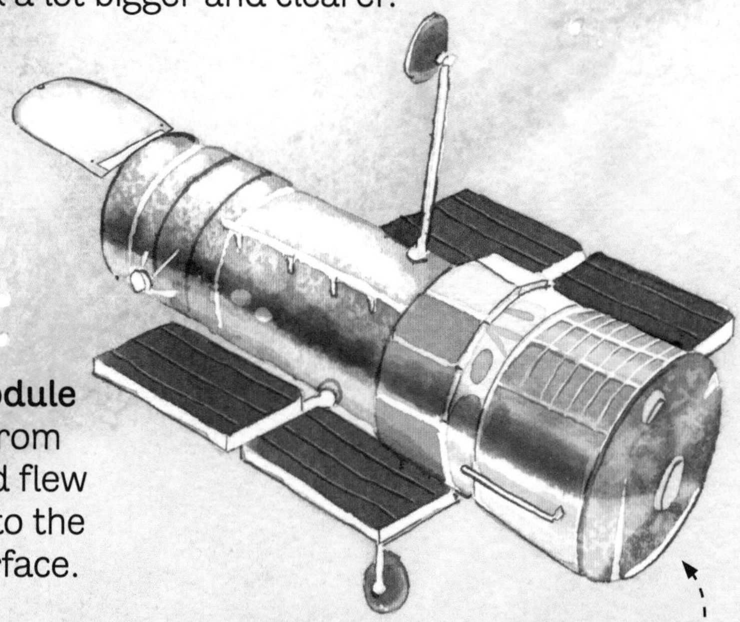

The **lunar module** separated from the **CSM,** and flew astronauts to the Moon's surface.

This is the **Hubble Space Telescope**. It was launched in 1990.

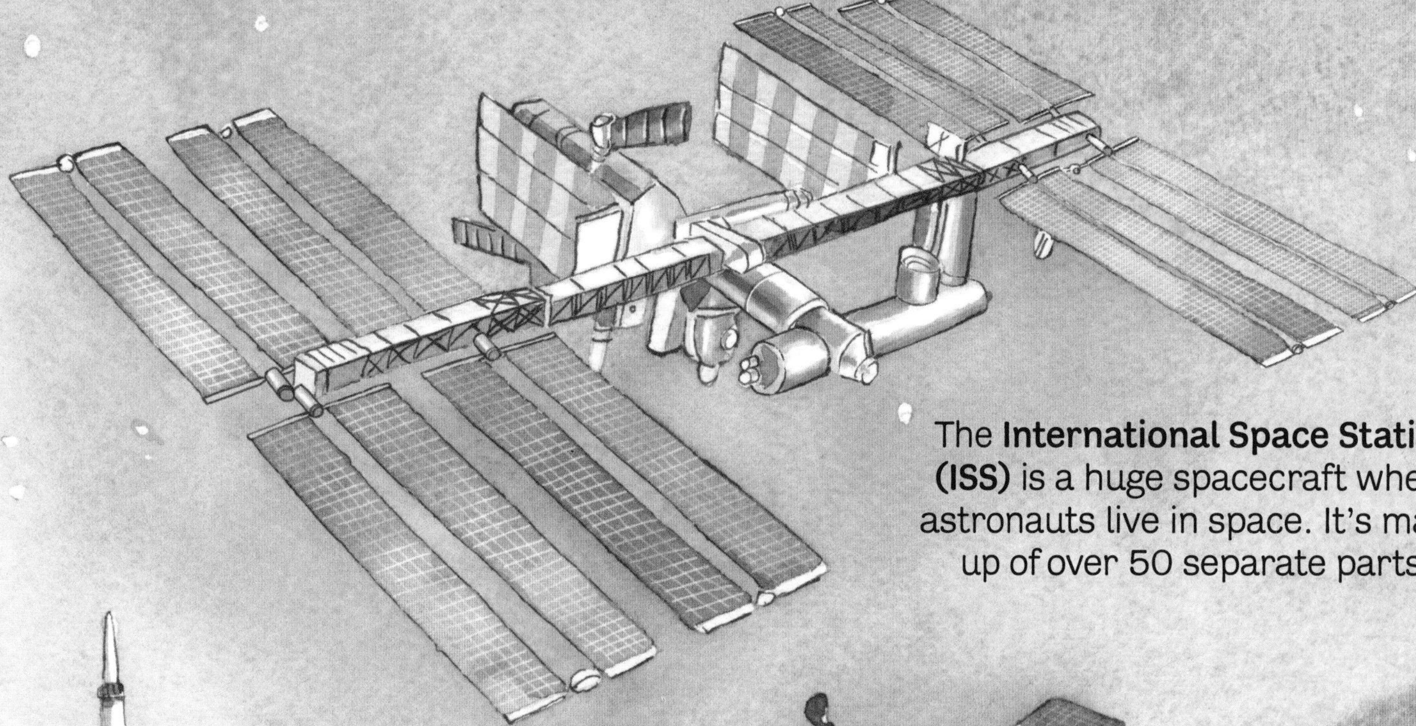

The **International Space Station (ISS)** is a huge spacecraft where astronauts live in space. It's made up of over 50 separate parts.

Launch vehicles are powerful rockets used to blast probes and other spacecraft into space.

Soyuz **spacecraft**

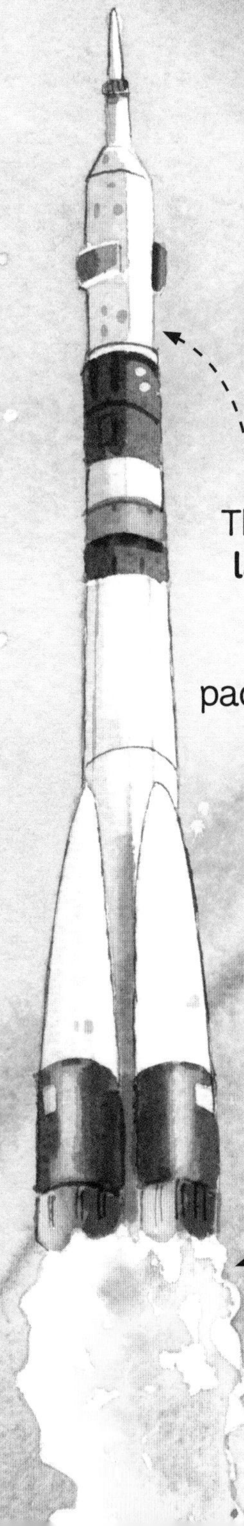

This is the ***Soyuz*** **launch vehicle**. The ***Soyuz*** **spacecraft** is packed inside here.

Hot, burning fuel pushes the rocket away from its launch pad.

Radio telescopes use big radio dishes to detect distant planets, stars and galaxies.

These are the **ALMA radio telescopes** in Chile.

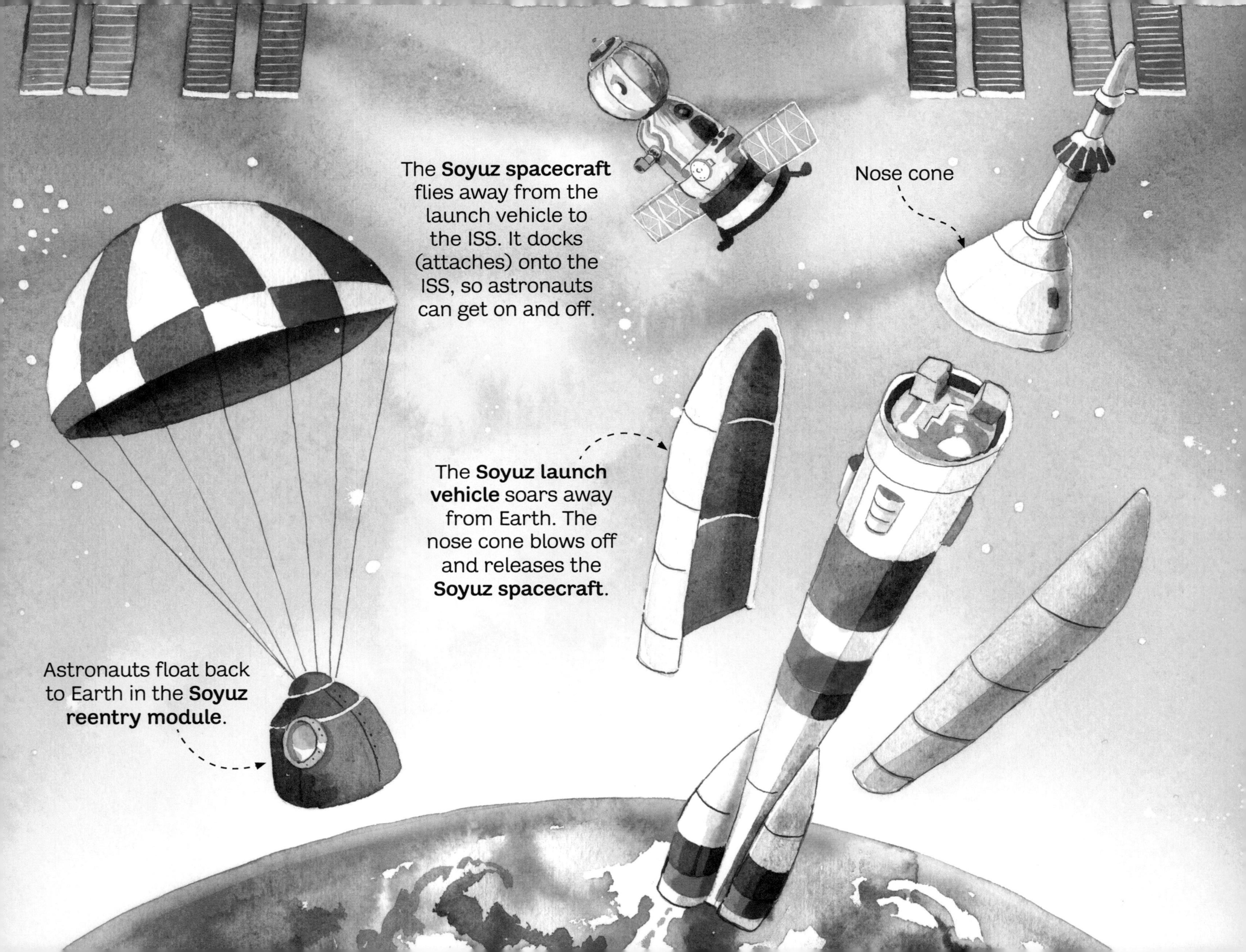
The **Soyuz spacecraft** flies away from the launch vehicle to the ISS. It docks (attaches) onto the ISS, so astronauts can get on and off.
Nose cone
The **Soyuz launch vehicle** soars away from Earth. The nose cone blows off and releases the **Soyuz spacecraft**.
Astronauts float back to Earth in the **Soyuz reentry module**.

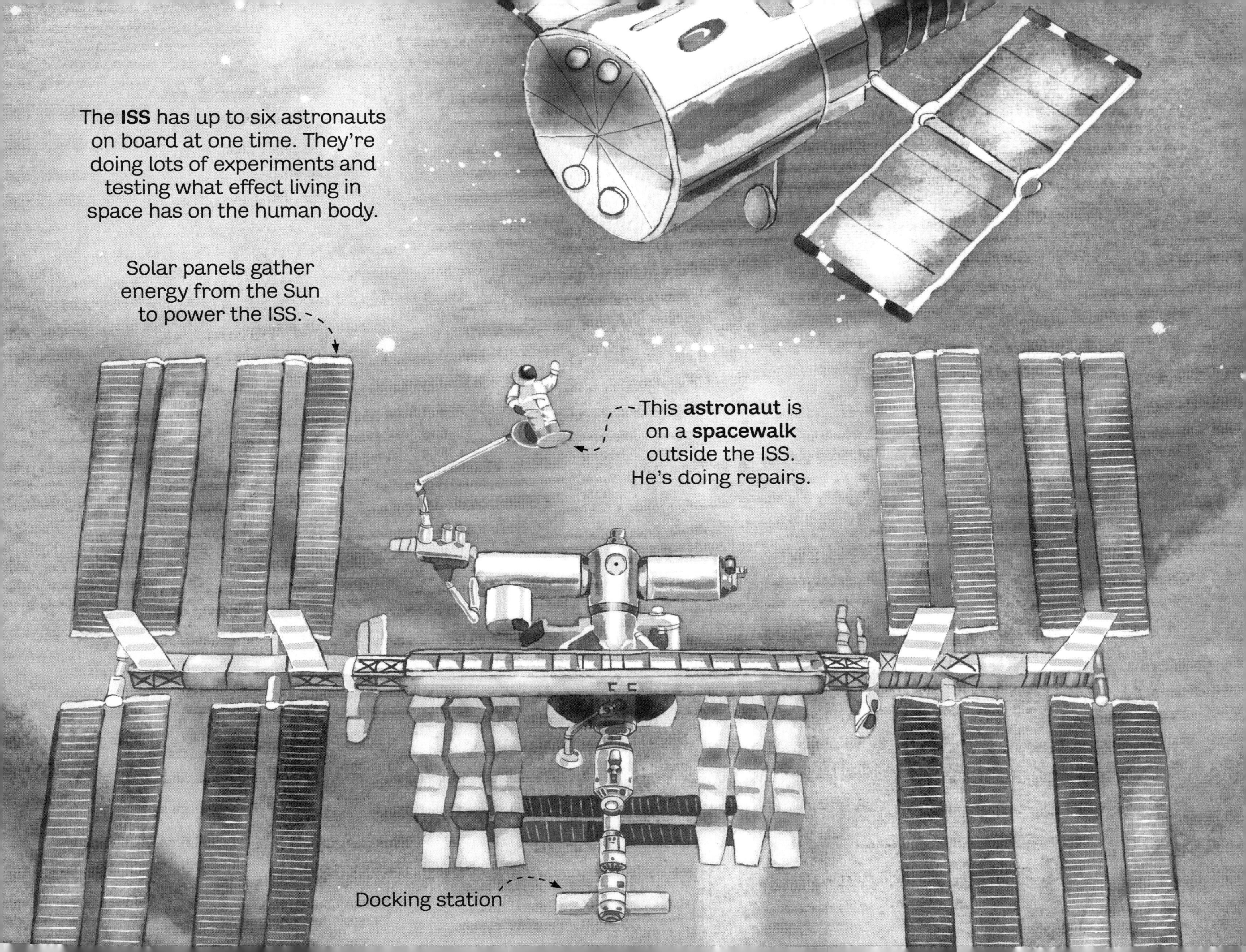
The **ISS** has up to six astronauts on board at one time. They're doing lots of experiments and testing what effect living in space has on the human body.
Solar panels gather energy from the Sun to power the ISS.
This **astronaut** is on a **spacewalk** outside the ISS. He's doing repairs.
Docking station

Roving around

The surface of Mars is cold, dusty and dry. But, scientists think that there was water there once, and maybe even life. They've sent robots to Mars to find out more...

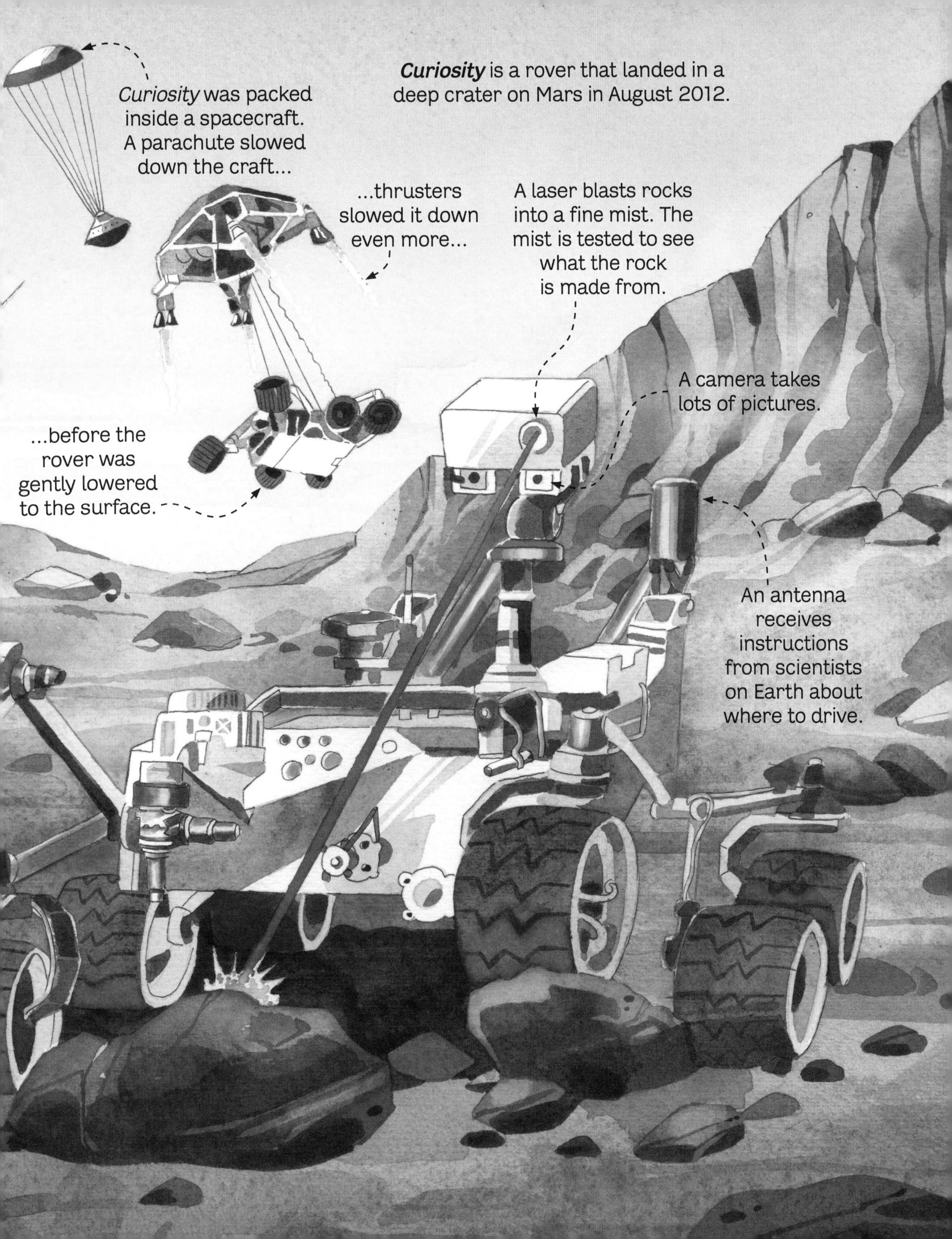
Curiosity is a rover that landed in a deep crater on Mars in August 2012.
Curiosity was packed inside a spacecraft. A parachute slowed down the craft...
...thrusters slowed it down even more...
...before the rover was gently lowered to the surface.
A laser blasts rocks into a fine mist. The mist is tested to see what the rock is made from.
A camera takes lots of pictures.
An antenna receives instructions from scientists on Earth about where to drive.

The night sky

If you look up at the sky on a clear night, you can see lots and lots of stars, and many other things, too.

Find out more about stars and planets by going to the Usborne Quicklinks Website at www.usborne-quicklinks.com and typing in the keywords *Big book of stars and planets*.

Series designer: Josephine Thompson Series editor: Jane Chisholm
Image manipulation: Nick Wakeford and John Russell Additional design: Will Dawes and Vickie Robinson

This edition first published in 2016 by Usborne Publishing Ltd., Usborne House, 83-85 Saffron Hill, London EC1N 8RT, England. www.usborne.com